Set Boundaries F

DRAWING THE RIGHT LINES

Staying Within The Zone Is What You Need

Paul Patton

Table of Contents

Chapter 1:

8 Signs You're An INFJ - The World Rarest Personality

Here are 8 signs that you might be an INFJ personality.

1. INFJs Often Report Feeling Lonely And "Different" — And For Good Reason.

INFJs are low in numbers so they tend to have trouble finding others who see the world in the same realm as they do. Most people who are this type have admitted feeling different from their peers since they were a very young child.

2. INFJs Take An All Or Nothing Approach To Life

INFJs, a curious mix of emotion and logic, don't like to waste their time on anything inauthentic. Although they may dabble in playing the field, INFJs are truly about quality over quantity and will become disinterested in anyone or anything they perceive as being fraudulent, scheming, or wishy-washy.

3. INFJs Exude Warmness, And Others Immediately Feel Comfortable In Their Presence

It's not uncommon for a stranger to sit down next to an INFJ and within minutes disclose their most personal secrets, fears, and dreams. In fact, this happens frequently to INFJs with seemingly no rhyme or reason. This personality type has a knack for making others immediately feel at ease, and they're great listeners and trusted confidants who speak in human terms and meet others where they are.

4. INFJs Are Somewhat Empathic, And They Tend To "Just Know" Things

One of my favourite one-liners from *Game of Thrones* is by the character Tyrion Lannister: "I drink and I know things." This can often be said of an INFJ, with maybe fewer libations. INFJs have a highly accurate sense of intuition that they've been sharpening all their lives. Without understanding exactly why or how, an INFJ will see, within minutes of meeting an individual, their true character. As a result, they tend to be more forgiving of their friends who exhibit unruly behaviour because they can identify the true root of it, such as insecurities or past trauma.

5. INFJs Ultimately Seek Genuine Truth And Meaning

This personality type does not care one iota about grandiose tales or extravagant gestures if there's not a true and genuine motive behind them. An INFJ's calling in life is to seek insight and understanding, and as they develop, they often can spot a lie or half-truth at a moment's notice. If they believe an individual to be a phony or a manipulator, they will have no trouble writing them off. Likewise, this type often enjoys traveling, adventures, and experiences that heighten their understanding of the intricacies of life and promote self-reflection.

6. INFJs Are True Introverts, Yet People Not Very Close To Them Believe Them To Be Extroverts

This happens because INFJs can be social chameleons and have an innate ability to blend into any social setting. The INFJ can be the life of the party for a night or two, showcasing their inviting nature and vivaciousness. However, this is never prolonged because, in introverted fashion, they lose energy when spending time with others. Those close to an INFJ know that this type prefers bars over clubs and barbecues over balls and can give a speech to thousands of people but cringes at the idea of mingling with the crowd afterward. Eventually, this type will need to retreat home for some quiet time to "recharge their batteries," or they will become on-edge and exhausted.

7. INFJs Have Intense, Unwavering Convictions, Sometimes To A Fault

An INFJ has certain ideas about the world and a need to foster change in society. These are deep-seated and intense beliefs that they will rarely abandon. If a career, relationship, or law does not align with their moral compass, an INFJ will have no qualms about ignoring it or leaving it in the dust.

8. INFJs Tend To Keep A Small Circle Of Friends And Prefer To Work Alone

Although an INFJ may have hundreds of acquaintances, if they call you "friend," you can be sure that they mean it for life. This type can count their close friends on a set of fingers, and they will be loyal and devoted to these prized individuals no matter how much time passes between their interactions. An INFJ can be a great team player, but the idea of group projects and meetings naturally make them sink down in their seat. These are people who enjoy working from home or in a quaint office with a handful of like-minded co-workers.

Chapter 2:

10 Habits You Must Stop If You Want To Manifest What You Want In Life

All of us have dreams that we would like to fulfill. What joy would it be to check our bucket list of wishes! However, there are obstacles on our way that could block the manifestation of our dreams. Here are ten habits that you must stop if you want to manifest what you want in life:

1. Lateness

A lot of people are struggling with timekeeping. What is even sadder is that we are normalizing lateness. Punctuality should be inculcated in our culture for the upcoming generations to understand the significance of observing time. People lose lifetime opportunities to the lateness in job interviews, business meetings, and client deadlines. Lateness demeans your character and casts you as unreliable before the clients and prospective employers.

2. Laziness

Laziness is a threat to personal and business growth. It is often disguised as selective participation, but it does not alter what it truly is. It has stagnated the dreams of many people because they were unwilling to go the extra mile. You cannot manifest your desires when you are lazy to pursue them. Manifestation requires hard work and aggressiveness. Do not be lazy to follow your passion and your efforts shall be rewarded.

3. Addiction

Addiction is being excessively used to something that you cannot do without. Although many people consider it normal, it is not one. It is the conditioning of the mind that you cannot perform in the absence of something else.

Addiction to anything can rob you of your breakthrough in life. It makes you a slave to the substance you are addicted to. Blue screen addiction or addiction to drugs or a close friend ties your progress to them. Fight it off to manifest your dreams.

4. Gambling

You can never gamble your way to wealth. Gambling is very addictive because it programs you to think that you cannot achieve anything unless you gamble. You can lose your possessions to gambling if you do not cut off this bad habit on time. As disastrous as gambling is, those affected may need external help to help them overcome it.

5. Wishful Thinking

It is good to have dreams about the future and the direction you would like to steer your life to. However, do not waste all your time in wishful thinking instead of actualizing your dreams. Building castles in the air should have a limit that is not crossed. Work on your vision for you to actualize it. No amount of wishful thinking will bring you closer to your dreams.

6. Jealousy

It is the root of most social problems. There is no need to be envious of other people's achievements. They worked hard to attain their current status and so should you instead of not wishing them well.

Learn to clap for others until your turn reaches. Celebrate their achievements and yours shall be celebrated too. Drop your jealous attitude because it will block others from celebrating you.

7. Keeping Bad Company

You should not keep any bad or negative company because they will influence you to be like them. Be mindful of the people you spend time with. They can sink your ambitions in hopelessness.

To manifest what you want, surround yourself with like-minded people who will support you. They relate to your dreams and can counsel you.

8. Negativity

Negativity has been silently killing the dreams of many people. You may have a viable dream that can be actualized with a little support but when you introduce negativity, it will only remain a dream. Manifestation requires positive confession and attitude. You need to believe that it can be done for you to achieve it. Even though everyone may doubt you, do not doubt yourself. Believe in yourself.

9. Fake Lifestyle

There is a thin line between a fake lifestyle and living your dream. The distinction between them is clearer when you consider the motive. The motive for a fake lifestyle is showing off while living your dream is genuine. Do not for anything else trade your dreams for a fake lifestyle. You will comfortably live within your means as you work for higher glory.

10. Blind Faith

It is most common between political leaders and their followers. Supporters of a political figure are often rubber stamps of what their leaders subscribe to. This is an unhealthy relationship because they blindly follow their leader even at the brink of perishing. You must stop blind faith in men for you to manifest your desires because people can disappoint you. You will get heartbroken and possibly abandon your dreams.

In conclusion, these ten habits have caused many people to stumble and fall never to recover soon enough to regain their crown of glory. Avoid them if you want to be successful.

Chapter 3:

8 Ways To Gain Self-Confidence

Confidence is not something that can be inherited or learned but is rather a state of mind. Confidence is an attribute that most people would kill to possess. It comes from the feelings of well-being, acceptance of your body and mind (your self-esteem), and belief in your ability, skills, and experience. Positive thinking, knowledge, training, and talking to other people are valuable ways to help improve or boost your confidence levels. Although the definition of self-confidence is different for everyone, the simplest one can be 'to have faith and believe in yourself.'

Here are 8 Ways To Gain More Self-Confidence:

1. Look At What You Already Achieved

It's easy to lose confidence when we dwell on our past mistakes and believe that we haven't actually achieved anything yet. It's common to degrade ourselves and not see our achievements as something special. But we should be proud of ourselves even if we do just a single task throughout the day that benefited us or the society in any way. Please make a list of all the things you are proud of, and it can be as small as cleaning your room or as big as getting a good grade or excelling in your job. Keep adding your small or significant achievements every day.

Whenever you feel low in confidence, pull out the list and remind yourself how far you have come, how many amazing things you have done, and how far you still have to go.

2. Polish The Things You're Already Good At

We feel confident in the things we know we are good at. Everyone has some kind of strengths, talents, and skills. You just have to recognize what's yours and work towards it to polish it. Some people are naturally good at everything they do. But that doesn't make you any less unique. You have to try to build on those things that you are good at, and they will help you built confidence in your abilities.

3. Set Goals For Yourself Daily

Whether it's cooking for yourself, reading a book, studying for a test, planning to meet a friend, or doing anything job-related, make a to-do list for yourself daily. Plan the steps that you have to take to achieve them. They don't necessarily have to be big goals; you should always aim for small achievements. At the end of the day, tick off all the things you did. This will help you gain confidence in your ability to get things done and give you a sense of self-appreciation and self-worth.

4. Talk Yourself Up

That tiny voice inside of our heads is the key player in the game of our lives. You'll always be running low on confidence if that voice constantly has negative commentary in your mind telling you that you're not good enough. You should sit somewhere calm and quiet and talk to yourself out of all the negative things. Treat yourself like you would treat a loved one when they tend to feel down. Convince yourself that you can achieve anything, and there's nothing that can stop you. Fill your mind with positive thoughts and act on them.

5. Get A Hobby

Find yourself something that really interests you. It can either be photography, baking, writing, reading, anything at all. When you have found yourself something you are passionate about, commit yourself to it and give it a go. Chances are, you will get motivated and build skills more quickly; this will help you gain self-confidence as you would gradually get better at it and feel accomplished. The praises you will get for it will also boost your confidence.

6. Face Your Fears

The best way to gain confidence is to face your fears head-on. There's no time to apply for a promotion or ask someone out on a date until you feel confident enough. Practice facing your fears even if it means that you will embarrass yourself or mess up. Remind yourself that it's just an experiment. You might learn that making mistakes or being anxious isn't half as bad as you would have thought. It will help you gain confidence each time you move forward, and it will prevent you from taking any risks that will result in negative consequences.

7. Surround Yourself with Positive People

Observe your friends and the people around you. Do they lift you and accept who you are or bring you down and point out your flaws? A man is known by the company he keeps. Your friends should always positively influence your thoughts and attitude and make you feel better about yourself.

8. Learn To Strike a Balance

Self-confidence is not a static measure. Some days, we might feel more confident than others. We might often feel a lack of confidence due to criticism, failures, lack of knowledge, or low self-esteem. While another time we might feel over-confident. We might come off as arrogant and self-centered to other people, and it can eventually lead to our failure. We should keep a suitable amount of confidence within ourselves.

Conclusion

Confidence is primarily the result of how we have been taught and brought up. We usually learn from others how to behave and what to think of ourselves. Confidence is also a result of our experiences and how we learn to react in different situations. Everyone struggles with confidence issues at one time or another, but these quick fixes should enough to boost your confidence. Start with the easier targets, and then work yourself up. I believe in you. Always!

Chapter 4:

Enjoying The Journey

Today I want to talk about why enjoying the journey of life is important. And why hurrying to get to the destination might not be all that enjoyable as we think it is.

A lot of us plan our lives around an end goal, whether it be getting to a particular position in our company's ladder, or becoming the best player in a sport, or having the most followers on Instagram or whatever the goal may be... Many of us just can't wait to get there. However, many a times, once we reach our goal, whilst we may feel a sense of satisfaction and accomplishment for a brief moment, we inevitably feel like something is missing again and we search for our next objective and target to hit.

I have come to realize that in life, it is not always so much the end goal, but the journey, trials, struggles, and tribulations that make the journey there worth it. If we only focus on the end goal, we may miss out the amazing sights along the way. We will ultimately miss the point of the journey and why we embarked on it in the first place.

Athletes who achieve one major title never stop at just that one, they look for the next milestone they can achieve, but they enjoy the process, they take it one step at a time and at the end of their careers they can look back with joy that they had left no stone unturned. And that they can live their life without regret.

How many times have you seen celebrities winning the biggest prize in their careers, whether it may be the Grammy's Album of the Year if you are a musician, or the Oscars Best Actor or Best Actress Award. How many of them actually feel like that is the end of the journey? They keep creating and keep making movies and film not because they want that award, even though it is certainly a nice distinction to have, but more so because they enjoy their craft, and they enjoy the art of producing.

If winning that trophy was the end goal, we would see many artists just end their careers there and then after reaching the summit. However, that is not the case. They will try to create something new for as long as people are engaged with their craft, as with the case of Meryl Streep, even at 70+ she is still working her butt off even after she has achieved all the fame and money in the world.

Even for myself, at times I just want to reach the end as quickly as possible. But many times, when I get there, I am never satisfied. I feel empty inside and i feel that I should be doing more. And when I rush to the end, I do feel like I missed many important sights along the way that would have made the journey much more rewarding and enjoyable had I told myself to slow it down just a little.

I believe that for all of us, the journey is much more important than the destination. It is through the journey that we grow as a person, it is through the journey that we evolve and take on new ideas, work ethics, knowledge, and many little nuggets that make the trip worth it at the end. If someone were to hand you a grand slam title without having you earned it, it would be an empty trophy with no meaning and emotions behind it. The trophy would not represent the hours of hard work that you have put in to be deserving of that title.

So, I challenge each one of you today to take a step back in whatever journey you may be on. To analyze in what aspects can you enjoy the moment and to not place so much pressure into getting to the destination asap. Take it one day at a time and see how the journey you are on is actually a meaningful one that you should treasure each day and not let up.

Chapter 5:

Enjoying The Simple Things

Today we're going to talk about a topic that might sound cheesy but trust me it's worth taking a closer look at. And that is how we should strive to enjoy the simple things in life.

Many of us think we need a jam-packed schedule for the week, month, or year, to tell us that we are leading a very productive and purposeful life. We find ways to fill our time with a hundred different activities. Going to this event, that event, never slowing down. And we find ourselves maybe slightly burnt out by the end of it.

We forget that sometimes simplicity is better than complication. Have you sat down with your family for a simple lunch meal lately? You don't have to talk; you just have to be in each other's company and enjoying the food that is being served in front of you.

I found myself appreciating these moments more than I did running around to activities thinking that I needed something big to be worth my time. I found sitting next to my family on the couch watching my own shows while they watch theirs very rewarding. I found eating alone at my favourite restaurant while watching my favourite sitcom to be equally as enjoyable as hanging out with a group of 10 friends. I also found myself richly enjoying a long warm shower every morning and evening. It is the highlights of my day.

My point is that we need to start looking at the small things we can do each day that will bring us joy. Things that are within our control. Things that we know can hardly go wrong. This will provide some stability to gain some pleasure from. The little nuggets in the day that will not be determined by external factors such as the weather, friends bailing on us, or irritating customers.

When we focus on the little things, we make life that much better to live through.

Chapter 6:

BE CONSISTENT, NOT PERFECT

It's often drilled into our heads that we have to be **great** at everything we do. It sounds like a lot of pressure, right? Well, what if the key wasn't in being great but simply showing up all the time, over and over?

Lasting progress isn't about being consistently great; it's about being great at being consistent. That means, instead of focusing on doing things perfectly, you simply focus on just the doing and getting better as you progress. When we focus on being consistent, we give ourselves more of an opportunity for greatness.

We're constantly seeing others online who are seemingly achieving greatness overnight leaving us feeling stuck. But what if I told you that the true power is in the process?

When we aim for consistency over perfection, these are the benefits:

1. You're Taken More By Those Around You

You can tell people until you're blue in the face what you **want** to do, but if you don't do it, they'll stop listening. However, if you show up every day and make a consistent effort, you'll be synonymous with what you're putting out there. Others will see from your actions that you're passionate about what you do or believe in.

2. You'll Make Progress

How many times have you prolonged doing something until it became practically nonexistent because you kept waiting for it to be perfect? It was a hard pill to swallow, but I found out that my <u>fear archetype</u> was the procrastinator a few months ago. I've always considered myself a perfectionist, and I find out procrastination is one of our key traits. We tweak things repeatedly, hoping to make them perfect, and end up never actually taking action. When we show up consistently, despite how perfect something may or may not be, we increase the possibility of progress.

By bringing more consistency into our lives, we'll have the opportunity to see true change in our circumstances. When we harp on perfection, it can often stunt our ability to grow. So, how do you become more consistent?

First, understand that you might mess up. And that's okay.
The biggest thing holding us back from being more consistent and instead relying on perfection is that we're afraid of making mistakes.

When we mess up, we feel discouraged, and a way of protecting ourselves is by trying to control the outcome. So, we wait until the time is perfect instead of taking the risk.

Allow yourself the space to be brave with your life. When faced with that fear, remind yourself that it's okay to make mistakes. To help, try reciting mantras like, "I may stumble, but I'll continue to learn and get better along the way."

3. A Small Step Is Always Better Than No Step at All

The most beneficial thing we can do for ourselves if we ever want to see change is to take action. Whether big or small, you are putting yourself out there, and doing the work consistently adds up. When we settle into the comfort of perfection, we stifle our potential.

So today or tomorrow, take one small action that will help move you in the direction you seek. And after that, do another small thing.

Along the way, praise your small wills and honor your process. With time and a steady effort, the things you desire will begin to manifest themselves.

Chapter 7:

Are You Trying Too Hard To Be A Perfectionist?

There's a fine line between having an achieving behavior and having a perfectionistic behavior. High achievers can be defined as determined, dedicated individuals who have a strong desire to accomplish important things. On the other hand, perfectionism has a flawed mindset that is driven by the avoidance of failure. True perfectionists don't try to be perfect but rather avoid not being good enough. This avoidance may dictate their behavior, leading to depression, anxiety, eating disorders, and even suicide.

Do you ever find yourself in a loop where you are scared of messing up even the tiniest of things? You keep obsessing over that essay over and over again to get it perfect, or you keep panicking over that outfit to get it right. Perfectionism manifests in many aspects of one's life. The stress of not being prepared or something not working out exactly as planned is perfectionism behavior.

Sure, this process may lead you to your desired outcome, like getting an A on that essay or causing someone in the hall to look twice at you. But the question remains, at what cost? How much did you stress over the smallest aspect of what you were trying to achieve? Was it the success that motivated you, or was it the fear of failure? And most importantly, are you being too hard on yourself?

The answer to all of the above questions is probably yes. We dive into everything so deeply that we forget there is no such thing as a perfect person. We are all full of flaws and mistakes. But still, we tend to strive for perfection, and we are looking to do things perfectly. And when it doesn't work out, it becomes detrimental to our progress and mental health. It would seem rather strange, but it is true that perfectionism can trigger procrastination, as the paralyzing fear that you will fail can stop you in your tracks. It's either if I can't do something perfectly, I shouldn't do it at all, or I have to wait for the perfect time to do this perfectly. This attitude would stop you from trying new things, putting yourself out there, or starting your tasks.

Being hard on yourself for trying to be perfect will worsen your mental health and affect your physical health. The blind pursuit of success can lead to neglect of your health and relationships. Recognize that no matter what the result will be, you have worked hard on your end. Acknowledge the efforts that you've put in reaching your goals. The work you do in achieving your goals is sometimes more important than the achievement itself. Find joy in setting goals rather than being weighed down by obligations.

Most importantly, get over it. Nobody's perfect, and you're no exception. Learn to accept your mistakes and flaws instead of holding yourself accountable for every shortcoming and keeping up your standards impossibly high.

Perfectionism is itself an imperfect way to look at life. Failing isn't the end of the world; and rather, it's the beginning of your success. You shouldn't let it get to you and stop you from pursuing your goals. Learn from the experiences and be kinder to yourself. You deserve it!

Chapter 8:

9 Ways To Know If You Are A Highly Sensitive Person

Being highly sensitive is personality trait that some of us may possess. Some people are born with it and some people are shaped by their life experiences, but whatever the reason is, it's there.

Barring all the articles and videos that you will find out there on this topic, my definition of a highly sensitive person is someone who has heightened emotions and sensitivity to the world around them. He or she is also a person highly driven by feelings and of the heart rather than the mind.

If you feel that you may be a highly sensitive person but aren't sure, we are going to explore today how we can identify the signs and traits of this unique personality. We will also address how you can manage your emotions when people come across too strong for your liking.

Here are 9 Ways To Know if You're A Highly Sensitive Person

1. You Pick Up On Subtle Emotional Cues

If you're a highly sensitive person, it is most likely that you're in tune with physical cues that regular people won't necessarily pick up on. Whether it is through someone's facial expression, your inner intuition towards an unfamiliar person, or picking up hints that someone is unhappy with you even though they try to hide it very well. Being highly sensitive allows you to have a strong radar and 6th sense on these things. More often than not, you are usually right on the money.

2. Other People's Tone Is Very Important To You

If someone's tone sets you off easily, you may be a highly sensitive person without realizing it. Tonality is very important to you, and you get easily put off when someone doesn't speak to you in quite the right way. Other people might have to be very careful when communicating with you and that could be a problem in relationships if people don't understand that side of you. Communicate to others that you may be offended without meaning it, but that you will just need some time to get past it if they are unknowingly triggering you in some ways.

3. You Are Driven by Intense Emotions

Does watching a sad movie make you cry but others around you don't? Or do you feel incredibly over-the-top happy while others around you simply feel like it was just alright? If you are a highly sensitive person, it is most likely that intense emotions are what drives you. You feel the extreme end of the spectrum. You may cry your eyes out in happiness or sadness, and that's perfectly fine. Embrace your feelings and don't change anything about you.

4. You Tend To Withdraw When Things Get Too Much To Handle

When things get incredibly overwhelming, do you feel a need to just crawl away and hide instead of facing the problem head on? When we are driven my intense emotions, sometimes it can work against us. We may feel bulks of sadness and fear that paralyses us from doing anything. If that is you, considering working through these emotions one step at a time and break down the problem you face into smaller chunks.

5. You Think Deeply About Things

If you have a tendency to question about life and your existence on this earth, you may be a highly sensitive person. As you are more in tuned with the world and the mind, inevitably philosophy will be something that you will naturally gravitate towards. Entertain these thoughts and express yourself in ways that celebrate your uniqueness.

6. People And Activities Drain You

If hanging out with large groups drain you more than they energize you, or if people's problems are not something that you can handle, you may be highly sensitive. Absorbing all the energy from others can be a very exhausting experience. If you need to, take a step back and spend time alone to recharge your batteries before putting yourself out there again.

7. There's No Middle Ground

You either feel incredibly happy or incredibly sad, there's no middle ground when it comes to your emotions. You either feel happy to be around someone or you just simply want to avoid them like the plague, you don't have the patience or tolerance to perform niceties to people you feel ambivalent about.

8. You Always Feel Misunderstood

Being highly sensitive could mean that you always feel that people don't understand you or are actually hearing what you say, even if in actual fact that they are and do. You always feel a need for reassurance and double confirmation that everything is heard loud and clear. Don't fall into the trap of having to over-defend your position on something if someone doesn't seem to see eye to eye on you on certain matters. It usually isn't their fault.

9. You Love Nature More Than People

Being around other humans can be exhausting for you if you absorb and feed off their energy all the time. Sometimes nature is one that revitalized and recharges you. You feel at home with the birds and the trees, the tranquility, and the peace that nature brings to you. Take time out of your schedule to visit the beach, parks, and gardens energize you and release all the built-up emotions that other humans and dumped on you.

Chapter 9:

8 Ways Journaling Will Change Your Life

Many renowned thinkers and innovators have one thing in common: journaling. Keeping a journal will transform your life in ways you never imagined. Whatever dilemma you are facing, the solution is always within you. And keeping a journal is a great way to figure this out. Once you start penning down your thoughts, you gain a deeper and more realistic view of your actual feelings.

Journaling is not primarily about keeping track of your day and remembering special moments. It is more of letting out or freeing your mind and penning those thoughts down. Journaling will reveal why you live, whether you are indulging in things you want to change or striving to make the changes you want to make.

Here are 8 ways journaling will change your life.

1. You Will Understand Yourself Better

Though many people, including writers, avoid keeping journals, the benefits of doing so cannot be overstated. One important advantage of journaling is that it allows you to gain a better understanding of what is important to you and what you want out of life. You learn more about yourself by keeping a journal that constantly reminds you of who you truly are.

2. Journaling Enhances Your Mental Health

Journal therapy is a legitimate, well-recognized method of counseling. Journaling has proved successful in stress, anxiety, depression management, and processing traumatic events. According to one study on the benefits of "focused expressive writing," journaling about traumatic, stressful, or emotional events several times enhances your psychological health, and thereof the overall sense of judgement and decision making.

3. Journaling Will Enhance Your Creativity

The notion that the brain system promotes learning manifests itself in increased creativity. Your increased activity, like journaling, will inspire your thoughts to connect and reconnect in whole new ways. There is no right or wrong way to journal, but if you want to be a writer, the pages of your journal can be your practice ground. Writing improves your ability to communicate, structure your language, and hence increase your creativity.

4. Journaling Creates Room for Self-Improvement

Journaling is an excellent way to keep track of your personal development. Writing down your experiences allows you to look back and assess your behavioral patterns and things to avoid or change. This will enable you concentrate on improving and becoming the better version of yourself. That way, you are more likely able to achieve your daily goals. Writing about positive reflections is also capable of boosting your confidence and self-esteem.

5. Journaling Is a Safe Place To Express Your Feelings

Journaling is a place where you can relent your emotions and still feel safe. You can hide it in a safe place only for your reach; hence no one will get the opportunity to share it or leave a negative comment like on social media. Write about your sadness, joy and frustrations, ease your mind off. You don't have to always keep it to yourself, journaling is your safe friend.

6. Stress Reliever

Journaling can be a good way to deal with everyday stress and anxiety. Each hemisphere of your brain contains almond-shaped cells called amygdalae, responsible for emotion regulation and memory encoding. When journaling becomes a daily habit, the amygdala recognizes it as a safe space for healing and reflection.

7. It Is a Strategic Way To Let Go of Your Past

One of the most essential aspects of journaling is that it will jumble your thoughts to the direction you need to take. The only way to get the best answers is to ask the right questions, and when you journal, you are able to do your consultation easily as you find your way to the next goal. Writing down how you feel can be the most effective way to let your emotions out.

8. Enhances Your Career

Journaling at work can help you focus and achieve your goals! Writing about work in your journal allows you to mark career goals and record your successes. Journaling adds a daily dosage of positivity to your day in the long haul.

Conclusion

Are you ready to start journaling? Good! Create a writing routine every day. Set aside 5 to 10 minutes and write about whatever is on your mind.

Chapter 10:

How To Worry Less

How many of you worry about little things that affect the way you go about your day? That when you're out with your friends having a good time or just carrying out your daily activities, when out of nowhere a sudden burst of sadness enters your heart and mind and immediately you start to think about the worries and troubles you are facing. It is like you're fighting to stay positive and just enjoy your day, but your mind just won't let you. It becomes a tug of war or a battle to see who wins?

How many of you also lose sleep because your mind starts racing at bedtime and you're flooded with sad feelings of uncertainty, despair, worthlessness, or other negative emotions that when you wake up, that feeling of dread immediately overwhelms you and you just feel like life is too difficult and you just don't want to get out of bed.

Well, if you have felt those things or are feeling those things right now, I want to tell you you're not alone. Because I too struggle with those feelings or emotions on a regular basis.

At the time of writing this, I was faced with many uncertainties in life. My business had just ran into some problems, my stocks weren't doing well, I had lost money, my bank account was telling me I wasn't good enough, but most importantly, I had lost confidence. I had lost the ability to face each day with confidence that things will get better. I felt that i was worthless and that bad things will always happen to me. I kept seeing the negative side of things and it took a great deal of emotional toll on me. It wasn't like i chose to think and feel these things, but they just came into my mind whenever they liked. It was like a parasite feeding off my negative energy and thriving on it and weakening me at the same time.

Now your struggles may be different. You may have a totally different set of circumstances and struggles that you're facing, but the underlying issue is the same. We all go through times of despair, worry, frustration, and uncertainty. And it's totally normal and we shouldn't feel ashamed of it but to accept that it is a part of life and part of our reality.

But there are things we can do to minimize these worries and to shift to a healthier thought pattern that increases our ability to fight off these negative emotions.

I want to give you 5 actionable steps that you can take to worry less and be happier. And these steps are interlinked that can be carried out in fluid succession for the greatest benefit to you. But of course, you can choose whichever ones speaks the most to you and it is more important that you are able to practice any one of these steps consistently rather than doing all 5 of them haphazardly. But I want to make sure I give you all the tools so that you can make the best decisions for yourself.

Try this with me right now as I go through these 5 steps and experience the benefit for yourself instead of waiting until something bad happens.

The very first step is simple. Just breathe. When a terrible feeling of sadness rushes into your body out of nowhere, take that as a cue to close your eyes, stop whatever you are doing, and take 5 deep breathes through your nose. Breathing into your chest and diaphragm. Deep breathing has the physiological benefit of calming your nerves and releasing tension in the body and it is a quick way to block out your negative thoughts. Pause the video if you need to do practice your deep breathing before we move on.

And as you deep breathe, begin the second step. Which is to practice gratefulness. Be grateful for what you already have instead of what you think u need to have to be happy. You could be grateful for your dog, your family, your friends, and whatever means the most to you. And if you cannot think of anything to be grateful for, just be grateful that you are even alive and walking on this earth today.

Next is to practice love and kindness to yourself. You are too special and too important to be so cruel to yourself. You deserve to be loved and you owe it to yourself to be kind and forgiving. Life is tough as it is, don't make it harder. If you don't believe in yourself, I believe in you and I believe in your worthiness as a person that you have a lot left to give.

The fourth step is to Live Everyday as if it were your last. Ask yourself, will you still want to spend your time worrying about things out of your control if it was your last day on earth? Will you be able to forgive yourself if you spent 23 out of the last 24 hours of your life worrying? Or will you choose to make the most out of the day by doing things that are meaningful and to practice love to your family, friends, and yourself?

Finally, I just want you to believe in yourself and Have hope that whatever actions you are taking now will bear fruition in the future. That they will not be in vain. That at the end of the day, you have done everything to the very best of your ability and you will have no regrets and you have left no stone unturned.

How do you feel now? Do you feel that it has helped at least a little or even a lot in shaping how you view things now? That you can shift your perspective and focus on the positives instead of the worries?

If it has worked for you today, I want to challenge you to consistently practice as many of these 5 steps throughout your daily lives every single day. When you feel a deep sadness coming over you, come back to this video if you need guidance, or practice these steps if you remember them on your own.

Chapter 11:

Figuring Out Your Dreams

Today we're going to talk about dreams and why it is important that we all have some form of a dream or aspiration that we can work towards.

For many of us who are educated in the traditional school system, we process from one grade to the next without much thought and planning besides getting into a good school. And this autopilot has caused many kids, including myself, to not have a vision of my future and what I would like to become when I grow up. We are all taught in some shape or form that we would need to choose a career and pursue that path. Dedicating years of higher education and hundreds of hours of curriculum work only to find ourselves hating the course that we had spent all this time and energy undertaking when we step into our jobs.

This has caused many to start doubting and questioning what we ought to really do with our lives and we might get anxious because this was certainly not part of the plan that we had set out since we were young.

What I have found personally is that I spent the time and effort to pursue a higher education not because I really wanted To, but rather to appease my parents that they did not waste all their time and money on producing me with proper schooling.

I did not however, go into my field of practice that I had spent the prior 3 years studying for. Instead upon graduating, that was when I really started to figure out what I really wanted to do with my life. Luckily for my parents, they were willing to give me the time and space to explore different possible passions and to carve out a path on my own.

I realized that as I started exploring more, and learning more about myself, the dream that I thought I once had started to change. Instead of dreaming of the perfect job and having the perfect boss, I now dreamt of freedom. To achieve freedom of time to pursue my passions, and to take steps that would move me one step closer to that dream as soon as possible.

Why this particular dream you ask? As I started exploring on successful people who have made it big in life, I realized that those that were truly happy with what they were doing, were not doing things for the money, but rather that they were able to quit their full-time jobs to pursue their interests because somehow, they had found a way to achieve time freedom that is irrespective of money. It amazed me how many found success by having the freedom to work from home, to not be bound by a desk job or to be hounded on their bosses. Some live for the climb up the corporate ladder, but I knew that wasn't going to work for me. And I knew I had to make something else work to survive.

So, I decided to dedicate my time and energy to only doing things that would help me achieve freedom and that became my dream to retire early and live off my past works.

The takeaway for today is that I want you to give yourself the chance to explore different things and take a step back to assess whether your current dream will actually serve you well in the long run, or if u don't even have a dream, whether you need to take time off to go find that dream for yourself.

I challenge each and every one of you today to keep an open mind that dreams can change, and you can always pursue a new path should you choose to. Because as the saying goes, the only constant in life is change.

Chapter 12:

8 Tips to Become More Resilient

Resilience shows how well you can deal with the problems life throws at you and how you bounce back. It also means whether you maintain a positive outlook and cope with stress effectively or lose your cool. Although some people are naturally resilient, research shows that these behaviors can be learned. So, whether you are going through a tough time right now or you want to be prepared for the next step in your life, here are eight techniques you can focus on to become more resilient.

1. Find a Sense of Purpose

When you are going through a crisis or a tragedy, you must find a sense of purpose for yourself; this can play an important role in your recovery. This can mean getting involved in your community and participating in activities that are meaningful to you so every day you would have something to look forward to, and your mind wouldn't be focusing on the tragedy solely. You will be able to get through the day.

2. Believe in Your Abilities

When you have confidence in yourself that you can cope with the issues in your life, it will play an important role in resilience; once you become confident in your abilities, it will be easier for you to respond and deal with a crisis. Listen to the negative comments in your head, and once you do, you need to practice replacing them with positive comments like I'm good at my job, I can do this, I am a great friend/partner/parent.

3. Develop a Strong Social Network

It is very important to be surrounded by people you can talk to and confide in. When you have caring and supportive people around you during a crisis, they act as your protectors and make that time easier for you. When you are simply talking about your problems with a friend or a family member, it will, of course, not make your problem go away. Still, it allows you to share your feelings and get supportive feedback, and you might even be able to come up with possible solutions to your problems.

4. Embrace Change

An essential part of resilience is flexibility, and you can achieve that by learning how to be more adaptable. You'll be better equipped to respond to a life crisis when you know this. When a person is resilient, they use such events as opportunities to branch out in new directions. However, it is very likely for some individuals to get crushed by abrupt changes, but when it comes to resilient individuals, they adapt to changes and thrive.

5. Be Optimistic

It is difficult to stay optimistic when you are going through a dark period in your life, but an important part of resilience can maintain a hopeful outlook. What you are dealing with can be extremely difficult, but what will help you is maintaining a positive outlook about a brighter future. Now, positive thinking certainly does not mean that you ignore your problem to focus on the positive outcomes. This simply means understanding that setbacks don't always stay there and that you certainly have the skills and abilities to fight the challenges thrown at you.

6. Nurture Yourself

When you are under stress, it is easy not to take care of your needs. You can lose your appetite, ignore exercise, not get enough sleep. These are all very common reactions when you are stressed or are in a situation of crisis. That is why it is important to invest time in yourself, build yourself, and make time for activities you enjoy.

7. Develop Problem-Solving Skills

Research shows that when people are able to come up with solutions to a problem, it is easier for them to cope with problems compared to those who can not. So, whenever you encounter a new challenge, try making a list of potential ways you will be able to solve that problem. You can experiment with different strategies and eventually focus on developing a logical way to work through those problems. By practicing your <u>problem-solving skills</u> on a regular basis, you will be better prepared to cope when a serious challenge emerges.

8. Establish Goals

Crisis situations can be daunting, and they also seem insurmountable but resilient people can view these situations in a realistic way and set reasonable goals to deal with problems. So, when you are overwhelmed by a situation, take a step back and simply assess what is before you and then brainstorm possible solutions to that problem and then break them down into manageable steps.

Chapter 13:

8 Facts About Quiet People

Quiet people often seem to be very misunderstood, and unless you're a quiet person yourself, it might seem odd that such people don't have very much to say. You may think people are quiet for several reasons. They're probably deep in thought. It could also be that quiet people are antisocial and lack the necessary skills to befriend others normally. However, there is still a lot that we don't really know about why quiet people are the way they are. To understand them a little better, here are 10 facts about quiet people.

1. They Learn Differently

Many people like to learn through interaction and conversations, but quiet people prefer to absorb information by observing everything. The art of observation takes plenty of skill as it requires the observer (or, in this case, the quiet person) to assess a person or a situation through appearances, mannerisms, and other indicators.

Imagine meeting someone new and trying to learn as much about them as possible only by observing their attire, body language, and level of eye contact. Quiet people have mastered this skill to understand their surroundings.

Of course, this method of learning is not enough to paint the whole picture. Quiet people will eventually speak up once they feel the need to know more about the person or the circumstances.

2. Quiet People Aren't Rude

Quiet people are often mistaken to be rude when it is often simply not the case. This tends to happen to introverts, who are naturally quiet and reserved when they meet others. However, just because their thoughts are not so apparent doesn't mean they are rude.

People have different interpersonal styles compared to their more social extroverted counterparts. Quiet people may just be taking their time to get to know you better before opening up more in conversations.

3. Quiet People Are More Observant

Have you ever wondered why quiet people know so much? It's because they are not distracted by the details of chit-chat. Instead, they carefully observe everybody and everything around them. Quiet people listen carefully and intently while paying close attention to details.

While louder people can dazzle people with their charm and energy, quiet people notice small cues and can easily tell whether they lack substance. This makes it easier for them to determine whether a person is honest or inauthentic.

4. Quiet People Take Speaking Seriously

Quiet people save their words and think carefully before saying anything. This may be because of a previous experience wherein they said the wrong thing at the wrong time, perhaps even to the wrong person.

Aside from being more careful about when to speak and what to say, quiet people hold different thoughts about speaking means compared to more talkative people. The latter may relate to other people better by sharing more freely; quiet people may not have the same approach.

5. They Are Curious About You

Quiet introverts are not fans of bragging about themselves, and they would much rather hear everything about the other person. Quiet people are naturally curious about others, including what motivates them and how they think and feel. This is why they seem always to want to listen rather than talk.

This is also what makes quiet people so wonderful — how often do you meet people who will genuinely give you their full attention because they want to hear what you say?

6. Quiet People Don't Necessarily Want To Be Alone

While quiet people prefer to keep to themselves or stay with a smaller circle, it does not necessarily mean that they want to be alone at all times. For instance, introverts use their quiet time alone each day to recharge their social battery before they go on to meet friends and family whose company they genuinely enjoy.

7.   Quiet People Are Good at Understanding

People who have less to say are often quite good at understanding people and various problems because they have learned the valuable skill of listening. While many people make the mistake of preparing their response to what someone else is saying, quiet people truly seek to understand without interruption.

8.   Quiet People Aren't Depressed

If someone silent and isolated must be depressed, right? Actually, quite the contrary is true; many quiet people are very happy individuals! It may seem like they are sad or withdrawn when they reject invitations to go out or sit on the periphery of social circles to listen to conversations. Quiet people are sociable differently, and they truly enjoy interacting with others without having very much to say.

Chapter 14:

7 Ways To Remove Excess Noise In Your Life

Ever felt lost in a world that is so fast paced, where no two moments are the same? Do you ever have a hard time achieving your goals, just because you have more distractions than a purpose to jump to success?

We live in a time, where technology is the biggest ease as well as the biggest difficulty while achieving our goals.

When you need something to be fixed, the internet can save us a lot of time, but the same internet can prove to be the biggest cause to take away the focus of the most determined too.

Although there are many important things on the internet too, that are essential to our daily lives, we don't need them at all times. Especially the realm of social media platforms.

Youtube, Facebook even Instagram can prove to be a beneficial tool for learning and teaching. But it can also make you spend more and more time on things that won't give you much except a good laugh here and there.

So what habits or activities can you adapt to distill these distractions. Reduce noise in life helping you focus better on the things that matter the most.

1. Divide your Tasks Into Smaller Ones

When you already have many distractions in life, including the household tasks and other daily life chores that you must attend to, then you must not avoid those.

But your dreams and goals must not be put aside at all, instead one must learn to complete them by dividing them into smaller, more manageable tasks.

Those who depend on you must have you when they need you, but that shouldn't stop you from doing what you require from yourself.

That can be done by keeping your head in the work whenever you get the chance to get maximum results from those short intervals.

2. Manage Your Time Smartly

Life is too short to be indulging in every whim and activity that you crave. Not everything or thought requires you to act upon.

A human being is the smartest being on this planet but also the stupidest. When a man or a woman wants to achieve something with all their heart, they do get it eventually. But when they have a thousand silly desires to go for, they slide off the set path as if there were none.

"You only Live Once".

Logically, this is a valid quote to get anyone off their path to success. But realistically this is also the most common reason for the failure of most of our youngsters.

You only get this life once, so you must go for the acts that bring you a better future with a surety of freedom without having to rely on anyone. Life doesn't need to be a continuous struggle once you use your energies at the right time for the right time.

3. Get Your Head Out of Social Media

I know this may sound a little Grownup and cliched, but we spend more time on our mobiles and laptops than going out and doing something physically in all our senses with our actual hands.

We can believe and act on anything that pops up on this screen, but rarely do we get anything worthwhile that we can adapt to change our lives once and for all.

Social media might be the new medium and source of knowledge and business for many, but for a layman, this is also the biggest waste of creative energy.

There is a lot out there to do in real life, a lot that we can realistically achieve. But, these days, we tend to hide behind a simple tweet and believe that we have done enough when the reality could have been much different.

4. Avoid Unhealthy Relationships

You might have always heard that a friend can be an emotional escape when you need one, but the excess of friends can prove to be the opposite of that. People seem to think, the more friends you have, the better you have a chance to stay engaged and have a happy social life. But this isn't always the case.

The more you have friends, your devotion gets scattered, and you find solace in everyone's company. This makes you more exposed, and people might take advantage of that. The fewer friends you have, the better loyalty you can expect and better returns of a favor.

When you have fewer friends, even if you lose one someday or get deceived, you would require less time to bounce back from the incident and you won't have to worry for long.

5. Get Out of Home Environment

Productivity required a productive environment. People tend to look for ease, but it doesn't always help us with finding our true potential.

You sometimes need a strict office environment or a more organized station or workplace. A place where there is no distraction or source of wandering thoughts to get your attention.

People need to understand how our brains work. If you cannot focus sitting in your bed, get a chair and a table. If that doesn't work for you, take a stool without a backrest. If you still feel at ease, just pick a standing table and start working while standing on your feet.

This makes your mind stay more focused on the task at hand to be done quickly.

6. Make A Schedule For These Distractions

If you feel like you can't give up the urge to pick your phone and check your feed. Or if you need to watch the last quarter of the league, or if you need to have a smoke.

Don't start fighting these urges. It won't help you, rather make things worse.

If you cannot let go off these things, it's fine. Make a deal with your brain, that you need this last page done within the next 10 minutes, and then I can go do what I needed direly.

You have to come at peace with your mind and work as a single unit. So, make time for these distractions and gradually you might be able to drop them once and for all.

7. You Don't Have to Compare with Anyone

Why do we humans need to compare and compete? Because we think it keeps our drive and our struggle alive. We think it gives us a reason and a purpose to go on and makes us see our goals more clearly.

Comparing to others won't make you see 'Your Goals', rather you would start creating goals that were never meant to be for you. You have these priorities just because you saw someone with something that appealed to you.

This is the noise and distraction that deviates you from the path that was meant to be for you all along.

If you want a clear vision of what you want, start removing cluttered thoughts, acts, and people from your life. It might seem hard at the start, but you won't have any regrets once everything comes in place.

Chapter 15:

7 Ways To Discover Your Strengths

It is a fact that everybody has at least one skill, one talent, and one gift that is unique to them only. Everyone has their own set of strengths and weaknesses. Helen Keller was blind, but her talent of speaking moved the world. Stephen Hawking theorized the genesis by sitting paralyzed in a wheelchair. The barber who does your hair must have a gifted hand for setting YOUR hair at reasonable prices—otherwise you wouldn't be visiting them.

See, the thing is, everyone is a prodigy at one thing or another. It's only waiting to be discovered and harnessed. Keeping that fact in mind…

Here are 7 Ways You can Discover Your Potential Strengths and Change Your Life Forever:

1. Try Doing Things That You Have Never Done

Imagine what would have happened if Elvis Presley never tried singing if Michael Jordan never tried playing basketball or if Mark Zuckerberg never tried coding. These individuals would have been completely different persons, serving different purposes in life. Even the whole world would've been different today if some specific people didn't try doing some specific things in their lives.

Unfortunately, many of us never get to know what we are truly good at only because we don't choose to do new things. We don't feel the need to try and explore things that we have never done before in our lives. As a result, our gifted talents remain undiscovered and many of us die with it. So, while the time is high, do as many different things you can and see what suits you naturally. That is how you can discover your talent and afterwards, it's only a matter of time before you put it to good use and see your life change dramatically.

2. Don't Get Too Comfortable With Your Current State

It is often the case that we cling on to our current state of being and feel absolutely comfortable in doing so. In some cases, people may even embrace the job that they don't like doing only because 'it pays enough'. And honestly, I totally respect their point of view, it's up to people what makes them happy. But if you ask me how one can discover their hidden talents—how one might distinguish oneself—then I'm going to have to say that never get used to doing one particular thing. If one job or activity occupies you so much that you can't even think of something else, then you can never go out to venture about doing new stuff. The key is to get out, or should I say 'break out' from what you are doing right now and move on to the next thing. What is the next thing you might want to try doing before you die? Life is short, you don't want to go on your whole life, never having experienced something out of your comfort bubble.

3.   What Is the Easiest Thing You Can Do?

Have you ever found yourself in a place where you did something for the first time and immediately you stood out from the others? If yes, then chances are, that thing might be one of your natural strengths.

If you've seen 'Forrest Gump', you should remember the scene where Forrest plays table-tennis for the first time in a hospital and he's just perfect at the game. "For some reason, ping-pong came very naturally to me, so I started playing it all the time. I played ping-pong even when I didn't have anyone to play ping-pong with.", says Forrest in the movie.

So bottom line, pay attention to it if something comes about being 'too easy' for you. Who knows, you might be the world's best at it.

4.   Take Self-Assessment Tests

There are countless, free self-assessment tests that are available online in all different kinds of formats. Just google it and take as many tests you like. Some of these are just plain and general aptitude tests or IQ tests, personality tests etc. while there are others which are more particular and tell you what type of job is suited for you, what kind of skills you might have, what you might be good at, and those kinds of things. These tests are nothing but a number of carefully scripted questions which reveal a certain result based on how you answered each question. A typical quiz wouldn't take more than 30 minutes while there are some short and long quizzes which might take 15 minutes and 45 minutes respectively.

Though the results are not very accurate, it can do a pretty good job at giving you a comprehensive, shallow idea of who you are and what you can be good at.

5. Make Notes On How You Deal with Your Problems

Everyone faces difficult situations and overcomes them in one way or the other. That's just life. You have problems, you deal with them, you move on and repeat.

But trouble comes in all shapes and sizes and with that, you are forced to explore your problem-solving skills—you change your strategies and tactics—and while at it, sometimes you do things that are extraordinary for you, without even realizing it. John Pemberton was trying out a way to solve his headache problem using Coca leaves and Kola nuts, but incidentally he made the world's coke-drink without even knowing about it. Lesson to be learned, see how YOU deal with certain problems and why is it different from the others who are trying to solve the same problem as you.

6. Ask Your Closest Friends and Family

People who spend a lot of time with you, whether it be your friend, family or even a colleague gets to see you closely, how you work, how you behave, how you function overall. They know what kind of a person you are and at one point, they can see through you in a manner that you yourself never can. So, go ahead and talk to them, ask them what THEY think your strongest suit can be—listen to them, try doing what they think you might turn out to be really good at, who knows?

7. Challenge Yourself

The growth of a human being directly corresponds to the amount of challenge a person faces from time to time. The more a person struggles, the more he or she grows—unlocks newer sets of skills and strengths. This is a lifelong process and there's no limit on how far you can go, how high your talents can accomplish.

Now, one might say, "what if I don't have to struggle too much? What if my life is going easy on me?". For them, I'd say "invite trouble". Because if you are eager to know about your skills and strengths (I assume you are since you're reading this), you must make yourself face difficulties and grow from those experiences. Each challenge you encounter and overcome redefines your total strength.

Final Thoughts

To sum it up, your life is in your hands, under your control. But life is short, and you got to move fast. Stop pursuing what you are not supposed to do and set out to find your natural talents RIGHT NOW. Once you get to know your strengths, you will have met your purpose in life.

Chapter 16:

7 Ways To Identify Your Weaknesses

We find ourselves asking this question perhaps a million times, "What am I good at?" and a question that follows right after that, "What am I not good at?" The list of the latter is much longer. We can't entirely blame ourselves for thinking that we have more weaknesses than strengths. Our cultures and society are too focused on the notion that we should overcome our deficits and weaknesses rather than appreciating and emphasizing our efforts and strengths.

While it is true that there are some people who are naturally talented and possess a high degree of willpower that surpasses those who make little to no effort, it is also true that a person can improve, or at least try to improve his shortcomings to his maximum level of potential.

Here are 7 ways to help you identify your weakness and tackle them properly.

1. Appreciate Yourself

The first and foremost thing to do is to give yourself a round of applause and pat yourself in the back. You have kept your ego aside and actually started taking action because deep down, you know that you suffer from some weaknesses too, and you are willing to improve them. It takes so many guts to admit to yourself this and to sit down and work on yourself. You are already a strong person. Way to go!

2. Analyze Your Daily Routine

From the minute you wake up to the minute you lay down and close your eyes, observe everything that you do in the day. Recall that whether you did something productive or wasted your whole day. See if you procrastinated your way out of the critical tasks that were assigned to you, or you simply called in a lazy day hoping that you would either start your work late or will do it tomorrow. Perceive your relationships too, what things are you lacking that's distancing you from your loved ones. Once you've listed out all of your problems, it's time to re-evaluate yourself.

3. Check Whether You Have A Negative Mindset

As we are programmed to consume negativity first, we tend to notice our faults and flaws and the people's weaknesses first. We become thoroughly convinced that no matter how hard we will try, there's always someone better out there who will do this job effortlessly. But this is an inaccurate approach as we should challenge ourselves, recognize our weaknesses, see where we are lacking, and then try to change ourselves for the better. The best method to identify our weaknesses is through self-evaluation. But sometimes, we do need a helping hand to advise us and assist us in improving our weaknesses.

4. You Doubt Yourself

After convincing yourself that you lack hard work and dedication in some specific areas, I.e., you're not giving priority to your dreams and goals, you're making excuses not to make any efforts, you're giving too much or too little of yourself in your personal relationships; this activity is taking a considerable amount of my energy, I don't feel optimistic about doing this work, there's always someone better out there who will excel me, I'll get it done, but I need more time for it. I'll sacrifice my happiness for someone else, and I won't say the things that are bothering me; I don't care enough to put up with their moods. So you find yourself making senseless excuses just to avoid doing your share of work.

5. Find Out What Is Holding You Back

It is time for you to find out what exactly is it that you're suffering with. Is it a lack of time? Procrastination? Boredom? Selflessness? Selfishness? You might be surprised to know that it's none of the above. Instead, we create these situations in our minds to help us cope with our wasted time and not feel guilty about our actions (victim-blaming). The only reason that you might be suffering from is laziness or maybe low self-worth. You automatically assume that since everyone is doing better than you, you don't need to improve yourself or save your energy on doing the tasks you have no interest in. You're draining out too much of your energy dealing with your personal life that it's now reflecting on your mental health too, and all in all, you have started considering yourself weak and vulnerable. You feel as if you're failing at life, and nothing makes you feel better.

6. Start Acknowledging Your Weaknesses

We are well aware of the fact that nobody's perfect. In fact, an ideal person is the one who knows that he is full of flaws and doesn't try to hide them, takes any criticism positively, and works hard to improve himself. A person who doesn't admit to his mistakes and weaknesses will end up alone and unsuccessful. It is best to know that all people have downfalls and to acknowledge them. One should self-evaluate as well as discuss with some closed ones about his shortcomings. For example, some people might say that you get furious very quickly and on petty things; that is one quality you wouldn't be aware of as such. Or maybe if you sit in a quiet, dark room and relive your life experiences, you might end up seeing a pattern of mistakes that you make every time.

7. Challenge Yourself

These mistakes might be the reason that you're not yet where you want to be in your life. Give yourself challenging and struggling situations and find solutions on how you would deal with them. Identify your areas of growth. See where you can make improvements. Sometimes, a particular activity or a particular relationship, or even a specific goal just isn't right for you, no matter how hard you try. Accept the fact with a big heart and open arms. Don't let yourself down and start working on the areas you can improve by dedication, passion, and hard work. Observe if you are actually making yourself better through your actions, or you're just only using words. As action speaks louder than words, make sure your efforts are improving your weaknesses.

Conclusion

We're more resilient than we give ourselves credit for. While it's undeniable that we all have weaknesses, and it takes a lot of nerve to admit to them, it's also true that one must accept them wholeheartedly and try to work towards betterment. Remember when you faced a strenuous situation, you felt like giving up because you felt so weak both physically and emotionally. But you rose from the ashes and got yourself out. Similarly, these weaknesses will try to bring us down at every step of our lives; we just have to make sure we don't succumb to them and keep our heads high. There's always room for improving ourselves and not to make our weaknesses and vulnerability get the best of us.

Chapter 17:

7 Simple Tricks To Improve Your Confidence

So many successful people acclaim their self-esteem and confidence for their success. But few people explain how to build confidence or how to become confident. It's hard because confidence is built on different things, but it's built on choices and achievements that fuel your passions and make you happy and proud of who you are. Exploring these is one of the most enjoyable activities of your life.

Here are a few ways to start building your confidence:

1. Get Things Done

Confidence is built on achievement. If you achieve significant and small goals, you will feel much better. It starts with your daily goal. What do you need to accomplish today and every day of this week or three days this week to help you reach your goal? If you hit the goals you've set for yourself every day, you'll most likely start to hit weekly and monthly goals, bringing you closer to your semi-annual and annual goal ranges. Remember that progress is incremental, and significant changes don't happen overnight. You will feel like you can take on a big project and set yourself a lofty goal because you think you can achieve it. Set a goal and do it.

2.   Monitor Your Progress

The best way to achieve your goals, big or small, is to break them down into smaller goals and track your progress. Whether you're trying to get a promotion, get a better job, go to college, change careers, eat healthier, or lose 10 pounds, the best way to know if you're making progress is to follow them. Try to quantify your accomplishments: how many job applications you apply for or go to college, what you eat and how much you exercise; write down any of your goals. It will keep you on track, and you will gain confidence in seeing your progress in real-time.

3.   Do The Right Thing

The most confident people live by a value system and make decisions based on it, even when it's difficult and not necessarily in their best interest but in the greater good. Your actions and decisions define your personality. Ask yourself what the best version of yourself you would like to be and do it. Even if it's tough and it's the last thing you want to do, and it means a short-term sacrifice on your part, in the long run, you'll love yourself more and be more proud of who you are.

4. Exercise

In addition to benefiting your overall health, exercise helps maintain memory, improves concentration, helps manage stress, and prevents depression. It's hard to worry when you don't have excess energy to absorb, and besides being uncomfortable at times, exercise improves all aspects of your life. So, stay active and make time to take care of yourself.

5. Be Fearless

Failure is not your enemy, and it is the fear of failure that paralyzes you. If you set big goals and dream big, you will feel overwhelmed and confident that you cannot achieve them. In times like these, you have to look inside yourself, gather every bit of courage you have, and keep going. All wildly successful people are afraid, and they keep working and taking risks because what they're trying to accomplish is more important and urgent than the fear of failure. Think about how much you want to achieve your goal, then put your worry aside and move on, one day at a time.

6. Follow Through

People respect people when they say they will do something, and they will do it. More importantly, you'll respect yourself if you say you'll do something and do it, and confidence will come more manageable because you know you don't mind the hard work. Actions give meaning to your words and will help pave the way for you to achieve your goals, strengthen relationships, and feel proud of who you are.

7. Do More of What Makes You Happy

What do you like to do in your spare time? Is it for hiking, kayaking, and enjoying the outdoors? Or do you live to lie on your sofa and watch all the great television available? Whatever you love, make space for it because life is short; you need time to enrich your life and rejuvenate yourself to be your best self.

Chapter 18:

7 Habits To Change Your Life

Consistently, habit drives you to do what you do—regardless of whether it's a matter of considerations or conduct that happens naturally. Whatever that is, imagine a scenario where you could saddle the power of your habits to improve things. Envision a day to day existence where you have a habit for finishing projects, eating admirably, staying in contact with loved ones, and working to your fullest potential. At the point when you have an establishment of beneficial routines, you're setting yourself up for a full, sound, and effective life.

Here are 7 habits that Can change your entire life.

1. Pinpoint and Focus Entirely on Your Keystone Routine

Charles Duhigg, in his power book stipulates the essence of recognizing your Keystone Habit—the habit you distinguish as the main thing you can change about your life. To discover what that is for you, ask yourself, what continually worries you? Is it something you would that you like to stop, or something you would do and prefer not to begin? The cornerstone habit is distinctive for everybody, and it might take a couple of meetings of profound thought to pinpoint precisely what that habit is.

3. Take the Challenges into Consideration

Challenges are regularly prompts that push you to fall once more into old habits. In the case of having to get to work earlier, your challenges may lie in your rest designs the prior night, or in organizing plans with a partner. These difficulties won't mysteriously vanish so you need to consider them. In any case, don't let the presence of challenges, or stress that new difficulties will come up later on, discourage you from setting up your new propensities. In the event that your difficulties incorporate planning with others, make them a piece of your new daily practice, as I'll clarify later. At this moment, basically recognize what the difficulties or obstructions are.

4. Plan and Identifying Your New Routine

Old habits never vanish; they are basically supplanted with new propensities. In the case of getting to the workplace earlier, the new standard includes going out a half hour sooner. On the off chance that the old habit was remunerated with the possibility that you'll have more energy for the day by remaining in your home longer, the new propensity needs to centre around the possibility that more rest doesn't really mean more energy. All in all, you'll need to address what you think you'll be surrendering by supplanting the old habit.

5. Reinforce a 30 Day Challenge.

By and large, your inability to minister beneficial routines basically comes from not adhering to them. A lot of studies show that habits, when performed day by day, can turn out to be important for your daily schedule in just 21 days. So set a beginning date and dispatch your game plan for a preliminary 30-day time span.

6. Empower Your Energy Through Setbacks

Here and there, it's not simply self-control that runs out. Now and then you are influenced from your ways by life "hindering" new objectives. In the event that something influences you from your test, the best game-plan is to assess the circumstance and perceive how you can get around, finished, or through that deterrent. Notwithstanding, when another propensity is set up, it really turns into our default setting. Assuming your standard habits are sound, unpleasant occasions are less inclined to lose you from your typical schedules. All in all, we're similarly prone to default to solid habits as we are to self-undermining habits, if those sound habits have become a piece of our ordinary daily practice.

7. Account Yourself and for Your Actions Publicly (Hold Yourself Accountable)

Your encouraging people are the most significant asset you will have at any point. Regardless of whether it's your closest companion, your accomplice or your Facebook posts, being responsible to somebody other than yourself will help you adhere to your objective. Simply remember that "responsible" isn't equivalent to "declaration". Anybody can advise the world they will rise ahead of schedule from here on out. However, on the off chance that that individual has a group of allies behind them, whom they routinely update, they are bound to stay with their new propensity during times when they are building up their new habit and inspiration is coming up short.

Chapter 19:

7 EASY WAYS TO BE MINDFUL EVERY DAY

Mindfulness has a way of sounding complicated. It's anything but. "mindfulness is paying attention in a particular way: on purpose, in the present moment, non-judgmentally," there are many simple ways you can be more mindful. Here are seven tips to incorporate into your daily life.

1. Practice Mindfulness During Routine Activities

Try bringing awareness to the daily activities you usually do on autopilot. For instance, pay more attention as you're brushing your teeth, taking a shower, eating breakfast, or walking to work. Zero in on the sight, sound, smell, taste, and feel of these activities. "you might find the routine activity is more interesting than you thought,"

2. Practice Right When You Wake Up

"mindfulness practice first thing in the morning helps set the 'tone' of your nervous system for the rest of the day, increasing the likelihood of other mindful moments." If you find yourself dozing off, just practice after having your coffee or tea. But "...don't read the paper, turn on the tv, check your phone or email, etc. Until *after* you've had your 'sit,'"

3. Let Your Mind Wander

"your mind and brain are natural wanderers – much like a crawling toddler or a puppy. And that's a good thing. Having a "busy brain" is an asset. "the beneficial brain changes seen in the neuroscience research on mindfulness are thought to be promoted in large part by the act of noticing that your mind has wandered, and then non-judgmentally – lovingly [and] gently— bringing it back,"

4. Keep It Short

Our brains respond better to bursts of mindfulness. So being mindful several times a day is more helpful than a lengthy session or even a weekend retreat. While 20 minutes seems to be the gold standard, starting at a few minutes a day is ok, too. For instance, you can tune into your body, such as focusing "on how your shoes feel on your feet in that moment, or giving attention to how your jaw is doing [such as, is it] tight, loose or hanging open at the audacity of the person in front of you in the coffee line?"

5.   Practice Mindfulness While You Wait

Waiting is a big source of frustration in our fast-paced lives – whether you're waiting in line or stuck in traffic. But while it might seem like a nuisance, waiting is an opportunity for mindfulness, halliwell said. When you're waiting, he suggested bringing your attention to your breath. Focus on "the flow of the breath in and out of your body, from moment to moment and allow everything else to just be, even if what's there is impatience or irritation."

6.   Pick A Prompt To Remind You To Be Mindful

Choose a cue that you encounter regularly to shift your brain into mindful mode. For instance, you might pick a certain doorway or mirror or use drinking coffee or tea as a reminder.

7.   Learn To Meditate

"the best way to cultivate mindfulness in everyday life is to formally train in meditation," practicing mindfulness is like learning a new language. "you can't just *decide* to be fluent in spanish – unless you already are – you have to learn the language first," "practicing meditation is how to learn the language of mindfulness." Meditation helps us tap into mindfulness with little effort. I suggest finding a local teacher or trying out cds.

Mindfulness isn't a luxury, "it's a practice that trains your brain to be more efficient and better integrated, with less distractibility and improved focus. It minimizes stress and even helps you become your best self." All of us have an emotional "set point." "some of us have more of a tendency toward withdrawal, avoidance, negative thinking and other depressive symptoms, [whereas] others have a greater tendency toward positive moods [such as, being] curious, tending to approach new things and positive thinking," through mindfulness, we may be able to train our brains and shift our set points. "mindfulness practice now has an abundance of neuroscience research to support that it helps our brains be more integrated, so your everyday activities, thoughts, attitudes [and] perceptions…are more balanced [or] well-rounded,"

Chapter 20:

6 Ways To Adopt New Actions That Will Be Beneficial To Your Life

There is this myth that goes around saying that, once you leave your teenage, you can never change your Habits. One can analyze this for themselves. Everyone has a list of new year's resolutions and goals. We hope to get these things done to some extent, but never do we ever really have a clear idea of how to get to those goals in the least possible time.

We always desire a better future but never really know how to bring the necessary change in our lives. The change we need is a change in attitude and behavior towards life altogether. Change is never easy, but it is achievable with some sheer willpower. You might be on the right track to lead a better life, but there are always more and better things to add to your daily habits that can be helpful in your daily life.

Here are 6 simple yet achievable actions you need to take:

1. Decide Today What Is Most Important In Your Life

Life is a constant search for motivation. The motivation to keep doing and changing for the better. Once you have something to change for, take a moment and envision the rest of your life with and without the change you are about to make.

If you have made up your mind, now think about how you can start off with these things. For starters, if you want a healthy lifestyle, start your day with a healthy breakfast and morning exercise on an empty stomach. If you want to scale your business, make a customer-friendly business model.

2. Make Reasonable and Achievable Goals

Adopting new habits can be challenging, especially if you have to change something in your day-to-day life to get better results. Start easy by making goals that are small, easy, reasonable, and won't give you a headache.

You can start off with baby steps. If you want to become more responsible, mature, and sorted in your life, just start your day by making your own bed, and do your dishes. Ride a bicycle to work, instead of a car or a bus. Things become smooth and easier once you have a reason for the hard acts.

3. Erase Distractions from Your Daily Life

You have wasted a lot already, don't waste any more time. As young as you are right now, you should feel more privileged than the older people around you. You have got the luxury of time over them. You have the right energy and pinnacle moments to seize every opportunity you can grasp.

Don't make your life a cluster of meaningless and profit-less distractions. You don't have to go to every public gathering that you are invited to. Only those that give you something in return. Something that you can avail yourself of in your years to come. Don't divulge in these distractions only for the sake of memories. Memories fade but the time you waste will always have its imprint in every moment that follows.

4. Make a Diary and a Music Playlist

You can devote some time to yourself, just to communicate with your brain and start a discussion with yourself. Most people keep a diary for this purpose, some people tend to make a digital one these days. When you start writing to yourself in the third person, talking and discussing your issues and your weaknesses, you tend to find the solutions within.

Most people find it comforting and calming when they have a playlist of music playing in the background while working. Everyone can try this to check if they get a better level of creativity if they have some small activity that soothes their stressed nerves.

5. Incorporate Regular Walk and Exercise in Your Life

When you know you have a whole day ahead of you, where you have to sit in an office chair for the next 8 hours. Where you have to sit in your home office looking at those sheets for most of the day. A 10 min walk before or after the busy schedule can help a lot in such conditions. You can never avoid physical activities for your whole life, especially if you want to live a healthier and longer life.

People always feel reluctant to exercise and running once they enter college or work life. Especially once they have a family to look out for. But trust me, your body needs that blood rushing once a day for some time. You will feel much more pumped and motivated after a hard 2-mile jog or a 15 min workout.

6. Ask Others for Help and Advice

You have a life to live for yourself, but always remember, you are never too old to ask for help. A human can never perfect something in their life. You will always find someone better than you at a particular task, don't shy to ask for help, and never hold back to ask for any advice.

We feel low many a time in our lives. Sometimes we get some foul thoughts, but we shouldn't ever pounce on them. We should rather seek someone's company for comfort and sharing our concerns.

Conclusion

The ultimate success in life is the comfort you get at the end of every day. Life can never be fruitful, beneficial, and worth living for if we don't arrange our lives as resourceful human beings. Productive minds always find a way to counter things and make the best out of everything, and this is the art of living your life.

Chapter 21:

6 Surprising Psychological Facts About Yourself

Understanding certain basic psychological realities about yourself, such as why we can't help but pay attention to sex and danger or that people see what they want to see, is crucial to figuring out what isn't working in your life. You probably know your favorite color, birthday, and cuisine, but wouldn't it be fascinating to understand psychological facts about yourself and how your mind works? You've come to the right place! Learning new things is always exciting, and this article will teach you some psychological facts about yourself that you probably didn't know! Continue reading to learn more!

1. You Can't Multitask

This is one of the psychological facts about yourself that has been discussed in several other articles. Many people believe they can multitask, but studies demonstrate that, except for a few physical acts like walking, the mind can only focus on one job at a time. You might be able to switch from one task to another quickly, but you can't focus on more than one at a time.

2. When You Read, You Anticipate

Do you ever find yourself reading aloud and speaking a word that isn't there? You predict the letters you'll receive and speak to them before you even see them. For example, you might read, "The tiny children play outside," but the text says, "The little children played out and about." When our minds put words together like "children play outdoors," we expect it; however, it isn't until we read it that we discover it doesn't say what we expect, such as "children play out and about." Try reading the following: I swear allegiance to the United States of Amsterdam flag. Many of you were aware of it, yet some of you responded with "America" since that is what your mind anticipated to see. Isn't it cool?

3. Synchronous Activity Bonds Your Group

Did you realize that performing activities as a group strengthens your bond? Have you ever pondered why cliques can be so powerful and close-knit, even if some members don't get along? They all sit together, eat together, laugh together, and move in unison! According to research, people who do activities simultaneously are more socially attached, more likely to make personal sacrifices for the group, and more likely to want to be around members of that group.

4. The Illusion of Progress Is Motivating

The apparition of development is quite enticing! According to a study, if you believe you're making progress toward a goal, you'll be more likely to achieve it. Example 1: You go to IHOP and are given a card with ten empty boxes to indicate how many times you've been there. On your tenth visit, you will receive a complimentary dinner. Example 2: You're given a card with 12 boxes, two of which are already filled in. Even though both cards require ten visits, studies suggest that people are more likely to complete the card with the 12 boxes faster due to the appearance of the development. Now that you're aware of this, you can devise some techniques to assist you in staying motivated and productive!

5. You Know How To Do Things You Have Never Done Before

It may appear that knowing how to do something you've never done before is a cool superpower, yet we're all capable of it. For example, your buddy claims that she can use her smartphone to scan the barcodes of foods and beverages to determine their nutritional content. Your brain generates an idea or picture of how to accomplish it and how it works, even if your phone doesn't have the capability or you've never done it before. This is called a mental model. A mental model is a person's mental representation of how something works. So, the next time you're faced with something new, whether technology or something else, you'll make some assumptions about how to use it!

6. Your brain Doesn't Rest When It's Sleeping

When we think about sleeping, we usually think of turning off the lights for the night. We sleep to get our minds off things or to help us make a choice, yet our minds are highly active while we sleep. Professor Matthew Wilson of MIT investigated sleep in rats and humans and discovered that we merge fresh memories and form new connections while we sleep. So pat yourself on the back; you're always working!

I hope you've learned a lot about the mind and its work! Which psychological truth piqued your curiosity the most?

Chapter 22:

6 Steps To Get Out of Your Comfort Zone

The year 2020 and 2021 have made a drastic change in all our lives, which might have its effect forever. The conditions of last year and a half have made a certain lifestyle choice for everyone, without having a say in it for us.

This new lifestyle has been a bit overwhelming for some and some started feeling lucky. Most of us feel comfortable working from home, and taking online classes while others want to have some access to public places like parks and restaurants.

But the pandemic has affected everyone more than once. And now we are all getting used to this relatively new experience of doing everything from home. Getting up every day to the same routine and the same environment sometimes takes us way back on our physical and mental development and creativity.

So one must learn to leave the comfort zone and keep themselves proactive. Here are some ways anyone can become more productive and efficient.

Whichever propensity you're chipping away at, pick each in turn. More than each in turn will be overpowering and will improve your probability of neglecting to improve any habits. Be that as it may, don't really accept that you can just change one thing about yourself; it's really the inverse. Dealing with this one Keystone Habit can have a positive gradually expanding influence into the remainder of your life also.

2. Recognize Your Present Daily Practice and the Reward You Get from It

Suppose you need to fabricate a habit for getting to the workplace a half hour early every day. You need to do this since you figured the extra peaceful time in the morning hours will assist you with being more gainful, and that profitability will be compensated by an expanded feeling of occupation fulfilment, and a generally speaking better workplace. As of now, you get to the workplace simply on schedule. Your present routine is to take off from your home in a hurry, at the specific time you've determined that (without traffic or episode) will get you to chip away at time. Your award is investing some additional energy at your home in the first part of the day, spending an additional half hour dozing or "charging your batteries" for the day ahead.

Everyone is always getting ready to change but never changing.

1. Remember your Teenage Self

People often feel nostalgic remembering those days of carelessness when they were kids and so oblivious in that teenage. But, little do they take for inspiration or motivation from those times. When you feel down, or when you don't feel like having the energy for something, just consider your teenage self at that time.

If only you were a teenager now, you won't be feeling lethargic or less motivated. Rather you'd be pushing harder and harder every second to get the job done as quickly as possible. If you could do it back then, you still can! All you need is some perspective and a medium to compare to.

2. Delegate or Mentor someone

Have you ever needed to have someone who could provide you some guidance or help with a problem that you have had for some time?

I'm sure, you weren't always a self-made man or a woman. Somewhere along the way, there was someone who gave you the golden quote that changed you consciously or subconsciously.

Now is the time for you to do the same for someone else. You could be a teacher, a speaker, or even a mentor who doesn't have any favors to ask in return. Once you get the real taste of soothing someone else's pain, you won't hesitate the next time.

This feeling of righteousness creates a chain reaction that always pushes you to get up and do good for anyone who could need you.

3. Volunteer in groups

The work of volunteering may seem pointless or philanthropic. But the purpose for you to do it should be the respect that you might get, but the stride to get up on your feet and help others to be better off.

Volunteering for flood victims, earthquake affectees or the starving people of deserts and alpines can help you understand the better purpose of your existence. This keeps the engine of life running.

4. Try New Things for a Change

Remember the time in Pre-school when your teachers got you to try drawing, singing, acting, sculpting, sketching, and costume parties. Those weren't some childish approaches to keep you engaged, but a planned system to get your real talents and skills to come out.

We are never too old to learn something new. Our passions are unlimited just as our dreams are. We only need a push to keep discovering the new horizons of our creative selves.

New things lead to new people who lead to new places which might lead to new possibilities. This is the circle of life and life is ironic enough to rarely repeat the same thing again.

You never know which stone might lead you to a gold mine. So never stop discovering and experiencing because this is what makes us the supreme being.

5. Push Your Physical Limits

This may sound cliched, but it always is the most important point of them all. You can never get out of your comfort zone, till you see the world through the hard glass.

The world is always softer on one side, but the image on the other side is far from reality. You can't expect to get paid equally to the person who works 12 hours a day in a large office of hundreds of employees. Only if you have the luxury of being the boss of the office.

You must push yourself to search for opportunities at every corner. Life has always more and better to offer at each stop, you just have to choose a stop.

6. Face Your Fears Once and For All

People seem to have a list of Dos and Dont's. The latter part is mostly because of a fear or a vacant thought that it might lead to failure for several reasons.

You need a "Do it all" behavior in life to have an optimistic approach to everything that comes in your way.

What is the biggest most horrible thing that can happen if you do any one of these things on your list? You need to have a clear vision of the possible worst outcome.

If you have a clear image of what you might lose, now must try to go for that thing and remove your fear once and for all. Unless you have something as important as your life to lose, you have nothing to fear from anything.

No one can force you to directly go skydiving if you are scared of heights. But you can start with baby steps, and then, maybe, later on in life you dare to take a leap of faith.

"Life is a rainbow, you might like one color and hate the other. But that doesn't make it ugly, only less tempting".

All you need is to be patient and content with what you have today, here, right now. But you should never stop aiming for more. And you certainly shouldn't regret it if you can't have or don't have it now.

People try to find their week spots and frown upon those moments of hard luck. What they don't realize is, that the time they wasted crying for what is in the past, could have been well spent for a far better future they could cherish for generations to come.

Chapter 23:

6 Signs You Were Born To Be A Loner

While the term loner has acquired certain negative connotations, it doesn't mean that being one is in any way undesirable. In fact, you are likely of higher intelligence than your more outgoing counterparts.

So here are 6 signs you were born to be a loner!

1. You're A Very Private Person

Doesn't matter what's happening, you could have gotten the biggest job promotion of your life, or you might have been struggling with your start-up, no one would ever know. You deal with the best and worst of times on your own, with no celebrations or consolations.

What's more, you don't feel the need to share these moments either. You might feel like it's completely unnecessary or just don't want to spend your energy on things like that. Either way, you're a private person and prefer to handle your affairs without dragging others into it.

2. You Like to Do Most Things by Yourself

Were you that kid in class who always preferred working alone? Did you always avoid group activities and projects? Are you that person who sits alone in a coffee shop? Being alone can really give you perspective on things and help you get organized, which is likely why you enjoy doing things by yourself.

Most people would feel awkward or embarrassed being seen alone at the movies or a restaurant. But you feel empowered, free, and relaxed doing things solo.

3. You Aren't Glued to Your Smartphone

In the age of social media and instant gratification, it's hard for people to put their phones down. But not for you. The last thing you want to do is share the tiniest details of your life with the entire world. So, whether you had an amazing pizza for lunch or are vacationing on an island, nobody would ever know.

You despise pointless phone calls and tiresome text messages, so you don't call or text unless necessary, and social media is pretty much useless to you.

4. You're Out of Reach for Long Periods of Time

Is your family used to you not answering your phone or dropping off the face of the earth? It used to worry them not being able to speak to you for days or months on end, but they now understand that your ability to socialize has its limits.

You simply don't feel so compelled to constantly stay in touch. So, if you aren't picking up your phone, you're just likely recharging by doing something you like, whether it's reading or doing art. For you, learning and creating stuff is a much more useful way to spend your time than catching up on the latest family news.

5. You Prefer to Work as A Freelancer

One thing you would never put on your resume is team player! There is nothing more tedious to you than working with a bunch of people, which is why a 9 to 5 will never be for you. The structures are too rigid, you have to play by too many pointless rules, and let's not even begin with office Christmas parties and signing those birthday cards.

You do your best work alone where you're in charge of the schedule and have 100 percent creative control.

6. You Don't Like Going To Social Events

Why spend New Year's in a group of drunk people yelling at the top of their lungs when you could easily spend the night on your own doing things you like? Most of the time, you think of a social event as something that eats up your time. That's because you value your time greatly and don't like wasting it on something you don't enjoy doing.

It doesn't necessarily mean you hate hanging out with your friends. It just means you want the interaction to be meaningful and not a fleeting moment aided by booze.

So, what do you think? Do you identify with any of these habits? If so, do you take them at face value or do you think they could be linked to a higher intelligence? What are some other habits that you think might be rooted in being intellectually gifted? Share your thoughts and comments below!

Chapter 24:

6 Signs You Need To Give Yourself Some Personal Space

While we wish to stay forever in the honeymoon phase of a relationship, we also must keep in mind that it is precisely what we call it; only a phase. Not every relationship is sunshine and rainbows every day. A relationship is between two individuals who both have individual needs. Sometimes, those needs include having some alone time with themselves. But how and when exactly do you know if you need some space from your partner?

April Masini, a New York-based relationship expert and author, says, "If you can't make it an hour or two without checking in or asking a question of your partner, you need a break." Needing space in your relationship does not in any way means that you don't love your partner anymore; it simply means that you need some time to get recharge and take care of yourself.

Here are some signs that you need to give yourself some personal space.

1. You Feel Stressed Out

Suppose you're unnecessarily stressed out, even if it isn't coming from your relationship. In that case, it's probably a good idea to spend some alone time and ponder over things. It can be some underlying tension coming from work or family, or it might be something in your relationship that you want but are not necessarily getting it. Taking some time out for yourself and figuring out where your stress is coming from or what's been upsetting you, you will then be better positioned to sort out your problems and discuss those issues with your partner.

2. You Don't Feel Like yourself

A significant sign indicating that you need some alone time for yourself is if you are started to feel exhausted, irritable, or simply just not yourself. Everyone should know the importance of needing some me time for yourselves. Your partner should understand if you need to take care of yourself and your mental health. Needing space from your partner in no way means that your relationship is at stake or if there's anything wrong with it. It simply means that you both need to spend time with yourself to rest, relax, or spend time with other people.

3. You Feel Suffocated

Spending so much time with people can prove fatal and can lead to being co-dependent on them, which is ultimately the kiss of death. It is assumed that, as a couple, you both should naturally be spending all of your time together, but there is such a thing as seeing too much of each other. It is essential to pull away and have some time for yourself. Find a hobby, take a walk, read a book. The more you spend your time with a person, the more likely you will get tired of each other soon. You need to get yourself some personal space not to get suffocated and overwhelmed by your relationships with other people.

4. You Don't Have any Outside Interests

Do you have any interests of your own, or do you rely entirely on the other person and their hobbies? It's healthy to have some things in common with your partner, but not all of them. Suppose you follow and copy their hobbies and interests and don't have any of your own. In that case, it might lead to some adverse psychological effects. Suppose they leave you or are just too busy to see you; you'll be left with nothing but boredom and waiting for the other person to catch up to you again. You need to give yourself space and find out what you like as an individual. Find your hobbies and passions, grow fond of them, and then work on them independently.

5. Spending Time With Them Is Draining You Out

If you aren't having as much fun as you used to have while meeting them, then you should take some space for yourself. If you're feeling drained out and low on energy after every interaction, it's time to spend some time apart. You get frustrated and irritated easily and don't make any efforts to resolve a fight. Patch-ups seem challenging for you; if your interactions are painful and difficult, then consider some alone time to gather your thoughts.

6. Your Vibe's Getting A Bit Off

Although there can be many reasons for this, stress, depression, exhaustion, etc., the primary cause can be that you're not getting enough space to deal with your emotions and feelings. Your relationship feels strained, and you feel like escaping from everything. This is the best time to ask for space from everyone and everything and ponder over whatever's bothering you.

Conclusion

Everyone deserves a relationship with more positivity than negativity in it. It's okay to need some space for yourself now and then. Evaluate your needs and try to figure out what you want.

Chapter 25:

6 Little Things That Reveal A Lot About You

It might be challenging to get to know someone. You think you've figured them out one minute, and then they show up as someone different from who you thought they were the next. Most of the time, people want to exhibit their best selves. Others are difficult to decipher. On the exterior, they may appear chilly, but inside, they're teddy bears. Perhaps they are a kind person in person but unpleasant behind your back.

Anyone you're attempting to read may also be trying to read you. Several small details may tell a great deal about your personality. For example, what kind of shoes you wear or where your gaze goes when sipping your coffee. If you're interested in learning more about the small details contributing to who you are, look no further.

Here are a few minor details that reveal a great deal about you.

1. Your Handshake

The handshake may reveal a lot about you regardless of your feelings towards shaking hands. Research from the University of Alabama in 2000 discovered that a person's handshake is consistent over time and is linked to personality traits. Those with a solid handshake are more outgoing, open to new experiences, and less neurotic. People who have a shaky handshake tend to make a wrong first impression. According to the study, women with a firmer handshake were also judged to be more liberal, intelligent, and open to new experiences.

2. How You Treat The Service Staff

Do you have a decent rapport with your waiter? What is your attitude about flight attendants? Or how about the receptionist? Keep an eye on how you and others treat individuals who work in the service industry. It might reveal a lot about their personality. Is your date making an effort to vent about your waitress? Is it true that they're losing their cool over nothing? And if they're friendly to waiters and staff while you're not looking, their friendliness is genuine. Pay attention; it may teach you a lot about individuals and how they deal with stress, even if it's only waiting for your chicken wings to come. So delectable.

3.

4. How Much Eye Contact You Make

Understandably, not everyone enjoys making eye contact. However, for some people, eye contact – or the lack of it – may disclose much about what they're thinking. According to Cornell University researchers, people commonly limit eye contact while discussing something humiliating or when they're deep in thought or emotion during a conversation. According to the research, if you're the one in the relationship which makes a lot of eye contact, you're probably the socially dominant one with a lot of confidence.

4. Your Email Etiquette

Your email handling style might reveal a lot about your personality. Text mining research has identified connections between particular terms and essential qualities, according to psychologist Tomas Chamorro-Premuzic. The phrases "I," "me," and "my" are more commonly used by narcissists. It demonstrates that someone is conscientious and a perfectionist if they don't have any errors. Poor grammar can also signify a lower IQ and academic intelligence. Long emails, although demonstrating thoroughness, might sometimes convey a sense of neediness.

5. How Late You Are

Many people believe that if you're always on time, you're a self-starter who is well-organized and driven. What if you're always late? People will probably think of you as a procrastinator or someone who doesn't give a damn. People frequently underestimate the time it will take to complete a task. This is referred to as the planning fallacy. According to research, people frequently underestimate the time it will take to finish a job by 40%. You might also be a multi-tasker if you're late.

6. Your Eating Habits

Do you consume your meal quickly or slowly? It may disclose a lot about your personality, believe it or not. The following is what the Huffington Post discovered after interviewing experts on food-related behaviors:
Slow eaters want to be in control and know how to appreciate life, whereas fast eaters are more likely to be ambitious, goal-oriented, receptive to experiences, and impatient. Picky eaters are more prone to be neurotic, whereas adventurous eaters are more inclined to move outside of their comfort zone.

Chapter 26:

5 Ways To Set Life Goals

Having goals for things we want to do and working towards them is an important part of being human. The path towards our goals may not always run smoothly or be easy, but having goals, whether big or small, is part of what makes life good. It gives us a sense of meaning and purpose, points us in the direction we want to go and gets us interested and engaged, all of which are good for our overall happiness.

Over 2000 years ago, Aristotle said "Well begun is half done." And with regards to goals, he's right (as he seems to have been on a lot of things). Paying attention to how we set our goals makes us more like to achieve them and achieving them makes us feel good about ourselves and our lives.

1. Decide

Think of something you want to do or work towards. It doesn't matter what, as long as it's something you want to do - ideally something you're interested in or feel excited by. It should be something you want to do for its own sake not for something or someone else. It can be a big thing or a small thing - sometimes it is easier to get going with something small. And it often helps if it's something that's just a little bit beyond what you currently can do - goals that stretch us can be motivating!

2. Write It Down Carefully

Writing down our goals increases our chances of sticking with them. Write down how you will know you have reached your goals and when you'd like to have achieved it by. Ask yourself: what it will 'look' like and how will you feel when you've done it? How does it connect to who or what you value in your life? Describe your goal in specific terms and timescales e.g. 'I want to plant lettuces, carrots and peas in the empty patch in my garden by the end of May' rather than 'I want to do some gardening.' Write your goals in terms of what you want, not what you don't want. For example: 'I want to be able to wear my favourite jeans again', rather than 'I don't want to be over-weight anymore'.

3. Tell Someone

Telling someone we know about our goals also seems to increase the likelihood that we will stick at them.

4. Break Your Goal Down

This is especially important for big goals. Think about the smaller goals that are steps on the way to achieving your bigger aim. Sometimes our big goals are a bit vague, like 'I want to be healthier'. Breaking these down helps us be more specific. So a smaller goal might be 'go running regularly' or even 'to be able to run around the park in 20 minutes without stopping'. Write down your smaller goals and try to set some dates to do these by too. Having several smaller goals makes each of them a bit easier and gives us a feeling of success along the way, which also makes it more likely that we'll stay on track towards our bigger goal.

5. Plan Your First Step

An ancient Chinese proverb says that the journey of 1000 miles starts with one step. Even if your goal isn't to walk 1000 miles, thinking about the first step on the way will really help to get you started. Even if you don't know where to start there's no excuse - your first step could be to research 'how to…' on the internet or think of people you could ask or to get a book on the subject from the library. Then think of your next step…and the next…

Keep going. Working towards our goals can sometimes be difficult and frustrating - so we need to persevere. If a step you're doing isn't working, think of something else you could try that still moves you forward, even a tiny bit. If you're struggling, ask people you know for their ideas on what you could do. They may help you see a different way. Thinking about different ways of reaching our goals makes it more likely we'll be successful. If you're really struck - take a break and then re-read the goal you wrote down when you started. If you need to adjust your goal - that's ok too. Then have another think about a small next step…

Celebrate. When you reach your goal take time to enjoy it and thank those that helped you. Think about what you enjoyed and learned along the way. Now, what is your next goal or project going to be?

Chapter 27:

Five Steps to Clarify Your Goals

Today, we're going to talk about how and why you should start clarifying your goals.

But first, let me ask you, why do you think setting clear goals is important?

Well, imagine yourself running at a really fast speed, but you don't know where you're going. You just keep running and running towards any direction without a destination in mind. What do you think will happen next? You'll be exhausted. But will you feel fulfilled? Not really. Why? Because despite running at breakneck speed and being busy, you have failed to identify an end point. Without it, you won't know how far or near you are to where you are supposed to be. The same analogy applies to how we live our lives. No matter how productive you are or how fast your pacing is, at the end the race, if you don't have clear goals, you will simply end up wondering what the whole point of running was in the first place. You might end up in a place that you didn't intend to be. Neglecting the things that are most important on you, while focusing on all the wrong things- and that is not the best way to live your life.

So, how can we change that? How can we clarify our goals so that we are sure that we are running the race we intended to all along?

1. Imagine The Ideal Version of Yourself

Try to picture the kind of person you want to be. The things you want to have. The people you want around you. The kind of life that your ideal self is living. How does your ideal self-make small and big decisions? How does he or she perceive the world? Don't limit your imagination to what you think is pleasant and acceptable in society.

Fully integrate that ideal image of yourself into your subconscious mind and see yourself filling those shoes. That is the only way that you'll be able to see it as a real person.

Remember that the best version of yourself doesn't need to be perfect. But this is your future life so dream as big as you want, and genuinely believe that you'll be able to become that person someday in the near future.

2. Identify The Gap Between Your Ideal and Present Self

Take a hard look at your current situation now and ask yourself honesty: "How far am I away now from the person I know I need to become one day? What am I lacking at present that I am not doing or acting upon? Are there any areas that I can identify that I need to work on? Are there any new habits that I need to adopt to become that person?

Be unbiased in your self-assessment as that is the only way to give yourself a clear view of knowing exactly what you need to start working on today. Be brutally honest with your self-evaluation.

It is okay to be starting from scratch if that is where are at this point. Don't be afraid of the challenge, instead embrace and prepare yourself for the journey of a lifetime. It is way worse not knowing when and where to begin than starting from nothing at all.

3. Start Making Your Action Plan

Once you have successfully identified the gap between your present self and your ideal self, start to list down all the actions you need to take and the things that need to be done. Breakdown your action plan into milestones. Make it specific, measurable and realistic. If your action plans don't work the way you think they will, don't be afraid to make new plans. Remember that your failed plans are just part of the whole journey so enjoy every moment of it. Don't be hard on yourself while you're in the process. You're a human and not a machine. Don't forget to rest and recharge from time to time. You will be more inspired and will have more energy to go through your action plan if you are taking care of yourself at the same time.

4. Set A Timeline

Now that you have identified your overarching goal and objectives, set a period of time when you think it is reasonable for a certain milestone to be completed. You don't need to be so rigid with this timeline. Instead use it as sort of a guiding light. This guide is to serve as a reminder to provide a sense of urgency to work on your goals consistently. Don't beat yourself up unnecessarily if you do not meet your milestones as you have set up. Things change and problems do come up in our lives. As long as you keep going, you're perfectly fine. Remember that it is not about how slow or how fast you get to your destination, it is about how you persevere to continue your journey.

5. Aim For Progress, Not Perfection

You are living in an imperfect world with an imperfect system. Things will never be perfect but it doesn't mean that it will be less beautiful. While you're in the process of making new goals and working on them as you go along, always make room for mistakes and adjustments. You can plan as much as you want but life has its own way of doing things. When unforeseen events take place, don't be afraid to make changes and adjustments, or start over if you must. Even though things will not always go the way you want them to, you can still be in control of choosing how you'll move forward.

As humans, we never want to be stuck. We always want to be somewhere better. But sometimes, we get lost along the way. If we have a clear picture of where we want to be, no matter how many detours we encounter, we'll always find our way to get to our destination. And you know what, sometimes those detours are what we exactly need to keep going through our journey.

Chapter 28:

5 Reasons Why Silence Is Powerful

For some people, silence comes naturally. These fortunate individuals know the power of silence and they are comfortable in that silence. There are quite a few of us who need to learn the art of practicing silence.

Read on for more reasons to try silence in your daily communications.

1. Silence Gets People's Attention

If you have ever been in a classroom or in a group situation you have most likely experienced how silence often gets everyone's attention. If the teacher or presenter is talking away the listeners' minds might start to wander. When the speaker stops talking a signal goes to the brain that something has happened. All of the sudden you pay attention to try and figure out why communication has stopped. The same is true in our daily conversations. If we are silent, people take note, and we gain their attention.

6. Silence Can Be an Obvious Answer

Sometimes when we communicate, we say too much. We over-explain. If a question is met with silence, there is often an answer in that silence. We can also soften the blow of a negative answer by silence being the response. There is an implied "no" without any harsh words or too many words that might do more harm than good. Another example is when someone says something we don't agree with or find offensive. If we are silent, we send a powerful message that communicates that we don't agree or are not going along with what someone is saying.

3. Silence Uses Nonverbal Language

Often our nonverbal language is a more powerful way of communicating than our verbal language.

4. Silence Offers Empathy to Others

There are times in life where silence offers empathy and understanding to others. Sometimes we don't have the right words to communicate to someone who is struggling with a hurtful or sorrowful situation. We can show someone we care, and we are there for them without using a plethora of words. We can offer comfort by our calming silence.

5. Silence Is Polite

We live in a society where we are constantly being barraged by noise and messages. From radio broadcasts, news channels, music in elevators, stores, and most businesses, to the rings of our phones, to the constant chatter of people around us. We often feel with so much going on we don't have enough time to communicate what we need to communicate. We are fighting with so many other sources of noise. When we do get the chance to talk, we usually feel like we have to cram every thought into a short span of time. However, when we are silent, we give others a chance to speak. We show them that they matter.

In conclusion, we can be effective communicators by utilizing our ability to be silent. There is great strength in silence. Now, we just need to keep practicing. Like the old adages go practice makes perfect and silence is golden.

Chapter 29:

Commit To A Specific Goal

A lot of us talk about what we are going to do. A lot of us have a lot on our to-do list that we are going to pursue or that we want to achieve. We all have ambitions, plans, goals, and dreams that we walk around telling everyone. But how many of us are actually doing something to achieve these goals?

The question we ask ourselves is that what are the things that we aspire to? What are the things that we want at no cost? What are the things that will bring us the ultimate happiness?

But none of us ask this; "What is the most important thing that I want to do today?".

The reality of this modern era is that we are busy with so many things that we don't have a clear image of anything anymore. Everything around us is going on and on and we are a slave to everything. Because we think that everything is equally important!

We want to have everything that the media showcases. We want all the glamour and all the success and every petty little thing. But none of us are actually getting any of that!

We need to have a discussion with ourselves once and for all; what is it that we are interested in, and what is it that we are committed to?

Let me clarify this a bit. You have a lot of things that you must do every day for a sustainable life cycle, but out of this daily grunt, what is that you are interested or curious to have, and what is it that must have at any cost?

I am sure you won't be able to come up with much! Because in life, not every stone is worth turning over. Not every tunnel is meant to be searched. Not every seed needs to be sown.

It's not bad to be curious about everything! Curiosity is what makes you set goals. But the reality is that you have one life and a small energy threshold. So why use it to gather everything? Why not put it all in just one basket at a time and let everything become somehow related to that?

If you are committed to a lot of things, you will try to master everything that doesn't even pair with any other thing. You will be distracted every hour of every day. Because you have put your eggs in so many baskets that you have lost count of the baskets.

But if you have one simple, yet important goal or dream, you will have a lot of time mastering a set of skills that complement each other at every step. This will not only increase your chances of getting to that goal but will also help minimize the time you need to reach that goal.

The less time it takes to achieve one, the more life you have ahead to plan and struggle for countless more goals.

Chapter 30:

3 Ways To Calm The Emotional Storm Within You

When emotions are already intense, it's often hard to think about what you can do to help yourself, so the first thing you need to work on is getting re-regulated as quickly as possible. Here are some fast-acting skills that work by changing your body's chemistry; it will be most helpful if you first try these before you're in an emotional situation, so you know how to use them.

1. Do A Forward Bend

This is my favourite re-regulating skill. Bend over as though you're trying to touch your toes (it doesn't matter if you can actually touch your toes; you can also do this sitting down if you need to, by sticking your head between your knees). Take some slow, deep breaths, and hang out there for a little while (30 to 60 seconds if you can). Doing a forward bend actually activates our parasympathetic nervous system – our 'rest and digest' system – which helps us slow down and feel a little calmer. When you're ready to stand up again, just don't do it too quickly – you don't want to fall over.

2. Focus On Your Exhale With 'Paced Breathing'

It might sound like a cliché but breathing truly is one of the best ways to get your emotions to a more manageable level. In particular, focus on making your exhale longer than your inhale – this also activates our parasympathetic nervous system, again helping us feel a little calmer and getting those emotions back to a more manageable level. When you inhale, count in your head to see how long your inhale is; as you exhale, count at the same pace, ensuring your exhale is at least a little bit longer than your inhale. For example, if you get to 4 when you inhale, make sure you exhale to at least 5. For a double whammy, do this breathing while doing your forward bend.

These re-regulating skills will help you to think a little more clearly for a few minutes, but your emotions will start to intensify once more if nothing else has changed in your environment – so the next steps are needed too.

3. Increase Awareness Of Your Emotions

In order to manage emotions more effectively in the long run, you need to be more aware of your emotions and of all their components; and you need to learn to name your emotions accurately. This might sound strange – of course you know what you're feeling, right? But how do you know if what you've always called 'anger' is actually anger, and not anxiety? Most of us have never really given our emotions much thought, we just assume that what we think we feel is what we actually feel – just like we assume the colour we've always called 'blue' is actually blue; but how do we really know?

Sensitive people who have grown up in a pervasively invalidating environment often learn to ignore or not trust their emotional experiences, and try to avoid or escape those experiences, which contributes to difficulties naming emotions accurately. Indeed, anyone prone to emotion dysregulation can have trouble figuring out what they're feeling, and so walks around in an emotional 'fog'. When you're feeling 'upset', 'bad' or 'off', are you able to identify what emotion you're actually feeling? If you struggle with this, consider each of the following questions the next time you experience even a mild emotion:

- What was the prompting event or trigger for the feeling? What were you reacting to? (Don't judge whether your response was right or wrong, just be descriptive.)

- What were your thoughts about the situation? How did you interpret what was happening? Did you notice yourself judging, jumping to conclusions, or making assumptions?

- What did you notice in your body? For example, tension or tightness in certain areas? Changes in your breathing, your heart rate, your temperature?

- What was your body doing? Describe your body language, posture and facial expression.

- What urges were you noticing? Did you want to yell or throw things? Was the urge to not make eye contact, to avoid or escape a situation you were in?

- What were your actions? Did you act on any of the urges you noted above? Did you do something else instead?

Going through this exercise will help you increase your ability to name your emotions accurately. Once you've asked yourself the above questions, you could try asking yourself if your emotion fits into one of these four (almost rhyming) categories: mad, sad, glad, and afraid. These are terms I use with clients as a helpful starting point for distinguishing basic emotions, but gradually you can work on getting more specific; emotions lists can also be helpful.